21st Century
Basic Skills
Library

YOUR HEALTHY PLATE
GRAINS

by Katie Marsico

Cherry Lake Publishing • Ann Arbor, Michigan

3

Published in the United States of America
by Cherry Lake Publishing
Ann Arbor, Michigan
www.cherrylakepublishing.com

Content Adviser: Theresa A. Wilson, MS, RD, LD, Baylor College of
Medicine, USDA/ARS Children's Nutrition Research Center, Houston, Texas

Photo Credits: Cover and page 1, ©Mircea BEZERGHEANU/Shutterstock,
Inc.; page 4, ©Monkey Business Images/Shutterstock, Inc.; page 6,
©My Portfolio/Shutterstock, Inc.; page 8, ©Alaettin YILDIRIM/Shutterstock,
Inc.; page 10, U.S. Department of Agriculture; page 12, ©iStockphoto.com/
rtiom; page 14, ©Fancy/Media Bakery; page 16, ©Elena Schweitzer/
Shutterstock, Inc.; page 18, ©iStockphoto.com/nicolesy; page 20,
©iStockphoto.com/CandyBoxImages.

Library of Congress Cataloging-in-Publication Data
Marsico, Katie, 1980–
  Your healthy plate. Grains/by Katie Marsico.
      p. cm.— (21st century basic skills library. Level 3)
  Includes bibliographical references and index.
  ISBN 978-1-61080-348-9 (lib. bdg.)—ISBN 978-1-61080-355-7 (e-book)—
ISBN 978-1-61080-401-1 (pbk.)
 1. Grain in human nutrition—Juvenile literature. 2. Cereals as food—
Juvenile literature. 3. Pasta products—Juvenile literature. I. Title.
II. Title: Grains. III. Series.
  TX393.M27 2012
  641.3'31—dc23   2011034537

Cherry Lake Publishing would like to acknowledge
the work of The Partnership for 21st Century Skills.
Please visit www.21stcenturyskills.org for more information.

Printed in the United States of America
Corporate Graphics Inc.
January 2012
CLSP10

TABLE OF CONTENTS

What Are Grains?

Do you eat cereal for breakfast? How about spaghetti for dinner?

These foods are made from **grains**. Grains are the seeds of certain grasses.

Farmers grow different kinds of grains. People use them to make food.

Some farmers grow wheat or rice in huge fields. Other farms grow barley or corn.

Cereal and pasta are two foods that are made from grains.

Bread and crackers are also grain **products**.

Grains such as rice and oats can be eaten by themselves.

Fruits

Grains

Dairy

Vegetables

Protein

ChooseMyPlate.gov

Why Do You Need Grains?

Grains are one of five main **food groups**. You should eat foods from all five groups.

Then you will have a **balanced diet**. It will help you stay healthy and grow!

Why Else Should You Eat Grains?

Eating grains helps keep you healthy by protecting against certain **diseases**.

Eating grains also helps your body produce more **energy**.

How Often Should You Eat Grains?

Someone your age should eat five **servings** of grains every day.

A slice of bread is one serving. So is half a cup of rice or pasta.

At least half of your servings should be whole grains.

Foods with whole grains use the entire grain seed.

Other grain products use only part of the seed.

Whole grains are better for your body!

Brown rice and oatmeal are made from whole grains.

So are popcorn and certain kinds of bread and pasta.

Talk to an adult about other healthy grain products.

How will you add grains to your diet today?

Find Out More

BOOK

Dilkes, D. H. *Bread and Grains*. Berkeley Heights, NJ: Enslow
    Elementary, 2012.

WEB SITE

**United States Department of Agriculture (USDA)—Food
Groups: Grains**
www.choosemyplate.gov/foodgroups/grains.html
Read more about grains and how to add them to your diet.

Glossary

balanced diet (BAL-uhntzt DYE-it) eating just the right amounts
of different foods

diseases (di-ZEEZ-uhz) conditions that cause health problems

energy (EN-ur-jee) strength needed to be active and alert

food groups (FOOD GROOPS) groups of different foods that
people should have in their diets

grains (GRAYNZ) the seeds of certain grasses that are used to
make food

products (PRAH-duhkts) items that are made to be sold

servings (SURV-ingz) set amounts of food

Home and School Connection

Use this list of words from the book to help your child become a better reader. Word games and writing activities can help beginning readers reinforce literacy skills.

a	brown	every	huge	part	talk
about	by	farmers	in	pasta	that
add	can	farms	is	people	the
adult	cereal	fields	it	popcorn	them
against	certain	five	keep	produce	themselves
age	corn	food	kinds	products	then
all	crackers	foods	least	protecting	these
also	cup	for	made	rice	to
an	day	from	main	seed	today
and	diet	grain	make	seeds	two
are	different	grains	more	serving	use
as	dinner	grasses	need	servings	what
at	diseases	groups	oatmeal	should	wheat
balanced	do	grow	oats	slice	whole
barley	eat	half	of	so	why
be	eaten	have	often	some	will
better	eating	healthy	one	someone	with
body	else	help	only	spaghetti	you
bread	energy	helps	or	stay	your
breakfast	entire	how	other	such	

Index

About the Author

Katie Marsico is an author of nonfiction books for children and young adults. She lives outside of Chicago, Illinois, with her husband and children.

ML

3—12